PRINCEWILL LAGANG

Crystal Bridges and Beyond: Alice Walton's Impact on Art, Business, and Philanthropy

First published by PRINCEWILL LAGANG 2023

Copyright © 2023 by Princewill Lagang

All rights reserved. No part of this publication may be reproduced, stored or transmitted in any form or by any means, electronic, mechanical, photocopying, recording, scanning, or otherwise without written permission from the publisher. It is illegal to copy this book, post it to a website, or distribute it by any other means without permission.

Princewill Lagang asserts the moral right to be identified as the author of this work.

First edition

This book was professionally typeset on Reedsy.
Find out more at reedsy.com

Contents

1	Introduction - Unveiling a Visionary Tapestry	1
2	A Vision Takes Root	3
3	Building Crystal Bridges: A Visionary Endeavor	6
4	Cultivating Cultural Connections: Alice Walton's Impact on...	9
5	Beyond Bentonville: Alice Walton's Influence on Business and...	12
6	Alice Walton's Cultural Catalyst: Nurturing Creativity and...	15
7	Legacy in Motion: Alice Walton's Enduring Impact	18
8	Bridging the Future: Sustaining the Legacy	21
9	The Uncharted Horizon: Exploring the Future of Cultural...	24
10	A Living Legacy: Nurturing the Seeds of Transformation	27
11	The Everlasting Legacy: Reflections on a Visionary Journey	30
12	A New Horizon: The Legacy Unfolding	33
13	The Evergreen Legacy: Nurturing Growth and Impact	36
14	Summary	39

1

Introduction - Unveiling a Visionary Tapestry

In the world of art, business, and philanthropy, few names resonate with the transformative power of Alice Walton. As the driving force behind Crystal Bridges Museum of American Art, her impact extends far beyond the realms of traditional museology. This book, "Crystal Bridges and Beyond: Alice Walton's Impact on Art, Business, and Philanthropy," unfurls the rich tapestry of Walton's visionary journey and explores the intricate threads that weave together her influence on cultural landscapes, philanthropic endeavors, and the intersection of commerce and creativity.

The story begins in Bentonville, Arkansas, where the architectural marvel of Crystal Bridges stands as a testament to Walton's belief in art as a catalyst for societal change. From the museum's inception to its dynamic evolution, the opening chapters unveil the narrative behind Crystal Bridges, tracing its roots and examining the profound impact it has had on the local community and the broader art world.

As the narrative unfolds, the focus expands beyond Bentonville, delving into the multifaceted dimensions of Walton's influence. Chapters dedicated to philanthropy showcase how the Walton Family Foundation has become a driving force in shaping educational systems, addressing environmental challenges, and fostering community development. The narrative then pivots to Walton's role as a cultural catalyst, exploring how her initiatives blur boundaries, foster creativity, and pioneer innovation in the intersection of art and technology.

Throughout the book, each chapter serves as a portal into a distinct facet of Walton's legacy. From the enduring impact of Crystal Bridges to the far-reaching initiatives of the Walton Family Foundation, the narrative navigates the intricate tapestry of Walton's vision, illustrating how it transcends conventional boundaries to touch the worlds of business, art, and philanthropy.

The later chapters peer into the future, contemplating the ongoing and evolving nature of Walton's legacy. As the book unfolds, it invites readers to explore uncharted territories, envision the perpetuity of philanthropic impact, and ponder the evergreen qualities of a visionary legacy that continues to shape cultural narratives, foster creativity, and transcend the boundaries of time.

Join us on this journey through the chapters that follow, as we unravel the layers of Alice Walton's impact and contemplate the enduring legacy of a visionary who has left an indelible mark on the canvas of art, business, and philanthropy.

2

A Vision Takes Root

Title: "Crystal Bridges and Beyond: Alice Walton's Impact on Art, Business, and Philanthropy"

The early morning sun bathed the Ozark Mountains in a warm glow as Alice Walton stood on the vast grounds of Crystal Bridges Museum of American Art. The air was filled with the promise of a new day, much like the transformative journey that Alice was about to embark upon. This chapter delves into the roots of Alice Walton's vision, exploring the intersection of art, business, and philanthropy that would redefine her legacy.

Setting the Stage

The chapter opens with a vivid description of Crystal Bridges, nestled in the heart of Bentonville, Arkansas. The architecture, inspired by the surrounding natural beauty, reflects Alice's commitment to seamlessly blending art with nature. As visitors stroll through the museum's corridors, the narrative unfolds, drawing attention to the carefully curated collection that spans centuries and captures the essence of the American experience.

CRYSTAL BRIDGES AND BEYOND: ALICE WALTON'S IMPACT ON ART, BUSINESS, AND PHILANTHROPY

The Walton Legacy

To understand Alice Walton's impact, it is crucial to delve into the roots of the Walton family's success. The chapter explores the history of Walmart, the retail giant founded by Alice's father, Sam Walton, and how the family's entrepreneurial spirit laid the groundwork for Alice's future endeavors. The narrative touches on the values instilled in her during her formative years and how they shaped her unique approach to art, business, and philanthropy.

A Personal Passion for Art

Alice's fascination with art didn't emerge overnight. This section delves into her personal journey with art, from childhood visits to museums to her travels around the world to explore different artistic traditions. The narrative highlights key moments where art became more than a passion for Alice—it became a vehicle for connection, understanding, and, ultimately, transformation.

The Genesis of Crystal Bridges

The chapter then shifts to the inception of Crystal Bridges, chronicling Alice Walton's decision to build a world-class art museum in Bentonville. The narrative explores the challenges she faced and the strategic decisions made to bring her vision to life. Interviews with key figures involved in the museum's creation provide insights into the early days of Crystal Bridges, from the initial concept to the grand opening.

Philanthropy in Action

As Crystal Bridges takes shape, the chapter explores Alice's commitment to philanthropy. It examines her belief in the power of art to inspire change and her dedication to making cultural experiences accessible to all. The narrative weaves together stories of the Walton Family Foundation's impact on education, community development, and the arts, illustrating how Alice's philanthropic efforts extend far beyond the museum walls.

Shaping a Legacy

The chapter concludes by foreshadowing the lasting impact Alice Walton is poised to make on the worlds of art, business, and philanthropy. It sets the stage for the subsequent chapters, which will delve deeper into specific aspects of her journey, from the evolution of Crystal Bridges to her influence on the broader cultural and business landscapes.

In "Crystal Bridges and Beyond," the reader is invited to step into Alice Walton's world—a world where art is not just a reflection of society but a catalyst for positive change. This chapter lays the foundation for a captivating exploration of the woman behind the museum and the transformative power of her vision.

3

Building Crystal Bridges: A Visionary Endeavor

Title: "Sculpting Dreams in Steel and Glass"

The Architectural Tapestry

The second chapter unfolds against the backdrop of Crystal Bridges' architectural marvel. The narrative immerses the reader in the design process, exploring the selection of renowned architect Moshe Safdie and his collaborative efforts with Alice Walton. Descriptive passages paint a vivid picture of the museum's innovative design, its organic integration into the natural surroundings, and the intentional juxtaposition of steel and glass against the lush Ozark landscape.

From Vision to Reality

The chapter delves into the challenges and triumphs of turning Alice's dream into reality. It takes the reader through the construction phases, from groundbreaking to the meticulous installation of artworks. Interviews with the project's key players, architects, builders, and curators provide a behind-the-scenes look at the complexities and triumphs encountered during the creation of Crystal Bridges.

Bridging Time and Space: The Collection

At the heart of Crystal Bridges is its collection—an expansive tapestry of American art that spans centuries. This section explores the curation process, detailing how Alice Walton and her team assembled a diverse collection that tells the story of America's cultural evolution. The narrative highlights key acquisitions, from iconic pieces to lesser-known gems, and how each artwork contributes to the museum's narrative.

The Grand Unveiling

As the museum nears completion, the anticipation builds to the grand unveiling. The chapter captures the excitement surrounding the opening of Crystal Bridges, from the inauguration ceremony attended by dignitaries to the reactions of the first visitors. Through anecdotes and interviews, the narrative conveys the emotional resonance of this cultural milestone and its significance for the local community and the art world at large.

Beyond the Museum Walls

Crystal Bridges is more than a static institution; it's a dynamic force for cultural engagement. This section explores the museum's educational programs, public outreach initiatives, and partnerships, emphasizing Alice Walton's commitment to making art accessible to diverse audiences. The narrative showcases the museum's impact on local schools, community groups, and the broader region, establishing Crystal Bridges as a catalyst for cultural enrichment.

Challenges and Controversies

No transformative endeavor is without its challenges. The chapter doesn't shy away from addressing controversies surrounding Crystal Bridges, from critiques of its location to debates over the funding model. Through balanced storytelling, the narrative provides a nuanced understanding of the complexities faced by Alice Walton and her team in realizing this ambitious project.

Legacy in Stone and Canvas

Chapter 2 concludes by reflecting on the enduring legacy of Crystal Bridges. The narrative considers the museum's role in redefining Bentonville as a cultural destination, its influence on the art world, and the lasting impact of Alice Walton's vision. As the museum doors open to the world, the reader is left with a sense of the profound cultural shift brought about by this visionary endeavor.

In "Sculpting Dreams in Steel and Glass," the reader is taken on a journey through the birth of Crystal Bridges—a journey marked by determination, collaboration, and a deep appreciation for the transformative power of art. This chapter serves as a testament to Alice Walton's unwavering commitment to shaping a cultural legacy that extends far beyond the physical boundaries of the museum.

4

Cultivating Cultural Connections: Alice Walton's Impact on the Art World

Title: "A Visionary's Palette: Redefining the Art Landscape"

Art as a Catalyst for Change

This chapter delves into the ways in which Alice Walton's vision extends beyond the confines of Crystal Bridges, exploring her impact on the broader art world. The narrative begins by examining her philosophy on art as a catalyst for societal change and the role museums play in shaping cultural narratives.

Expanding the Canvas: Acquisitions and Exhibitions

A significant portion of the chapter focuses on Alice Walton's role as a patron of the arts. It takes the reader on a journey through the expansion of the Crystal Bridges collection, spotlighting key acquisitions and notable exhibitions that have left an indelible mark on the art world. Interviews with curators, artists, and art historians provide insights into the curatorial decisions that have shaped the museum's identity.

Nurturing Living Artists

Alice Walton's commitment to living artists is explored in this section, shedding light on her support for contemporary art and emerging talents. The narrative examines initiatives, grants, and residencies sponsored by the Walton Family Foundation that contribute to the cultivation of a vibrant and diverse artistic landscape.

Breaking Barriers: Inclusivity in the Arts

This section tackles Alice Walton's dedication to promoting inclusivity in the arts. It explores initiatives aimed at breaking down barriers to access, fostering diversity in museum leadership, and supporting underrepresented voices in the art community. Interviews with individuals involved in these programs provide a firsthand account of the positive impact of Walton's initiatives.

Global Dialogues: Art and Diplomacy

The narrative widens its focus to explore Alice Walton's role in fostering international cultural exchanges. It highlights collaborations between Crystal Bridges and global institutions, showcasing how art can be a powerful tool for diplomatic engagement and cross-cultural dialogue. Through anecdotes and case studies, the chapter illustrates the ripple effect of these collaborations on the global stage.

Shaping the Future: Educational Initiatives

The chapter shifts to Alice Walton's commitment to arts education. It explores the development of educational programs at Crystal Bridges and initiatives supported by the Walton Family Foundation aimed at integrating the arts into school curricula. Through interviews with educators, the narrative underscores the transformative impact of arts education on students and communities.

Challenges and Critiques: A Reflective Stance

No exploration of Alice Walton's impact on the art world would be complete without addressing criticisms and challenges. The narrative provides a balanced perspective on controversies, addressing issues such as the commodification of art, the role of philanthropy in the arts, and debates surrounding cultural appropriation. It portrays Alice Walton as a figure willing to engage in dialogue and evolve in response to the evolving landscape.

A Lasting Legacy

Chapter 3 concludes by synthesizing the various facets of Alice Walton's influence on the art world. It reflects on the interconnectedness of her philanthropic efforts, the vibrancy of Crystal Bridges, and the far-reaching implications of her vision. The reader is left with a sense of the enduring impact of Alice Walton's contributions to the cultural fabric of society.

In "A Visionary's Palette: Redefining the Art Landscape," the reader is invited to explore the multifaceted ways in which Alice Walton's passion for art transcends the walls of Crystal Bridges, leaving an indelible mark on the global art scene. This chapter celebrates her role as a catalyst for change, shaping the narrative of art as a force for positive transformation.

5

Beyond Bentonville: Alice Walton's Influence on Business and Philanthropy

Title: "Ventures in Vision: Blurring Boundaries, Expanding Impact"

A Philanthropic Landscape

This chapter delves into Alice Walton's impact on the philanthropic sector, exploring the evolution of the Walton Family Foundation and its multifaceted initiatives. It provides a comprehensive overview of the foundation's focus areas, from education and environmental conservation to healthcare and community development.

Trailblazing Philanthropy: Education Initiatives

The narrative shines a spotlight on Alice Walton's commitment to education. It explores the Walton Family Foundation's initiatives aimed at improving educational outcomes, fostering innovation in schools, and addressing systemic challenges in the education system. Interviews with educators, policymakers, and community leaders offer a nuanced perspective on the foundation's role in shaping educational landscapes.

Sustaining the Earth: Environmental Conservation

This section explores Alice Walton's dedication to environmental stewardship. The narrative examines the Walton Family Foundation's efforts to support sustainable practices, conserve natural resources, and address pressing environmental challenges. Case studies and interviews with environmentalists provide insights into the foundation's role in promoting responsible and impactful conservation initiatives.

Bridging Healthcare Gaps

The chapter shifts focus to Alice Walton's influence on healthcare philanthropy. It explores initiatives aimed at improving healthcare access, supporting medical research, and addressing health disparities. Through personal stories and expert interviews, the narrative highlights the foundation's role in shaping healthcare policies and fostering innovations in the healthcare sector.

Blurring Boundaries: The Intersection of Business and Philanthropy

This section explores the unique intersection of Alice Walton's business acumen and philanthropic endeavors. It examines how her experiences in the business world, particularly as part of the Walton family and Walmart legacy, have informed her approach to philanthropy. Interviews with business leaders and philanthropists provide insights into the synergies between commerce and giving back.

The Ripple Effect: Community Development

The narrative expands to Alice Walton's impact on community development, examining how the Walton Family Foundation has played a pivotal role in revitalizing communities. Case studies of community-led projects and interviews with local leaders illustrate the foundation's commitment to empowering communities and fostering sustainable development.

Challenges and Reflections: Navigating Complexities

No exploration of Alice Walton's philanthropic impact would be complete without addressing challenges and critiques. This section navigates the complexities of philanthropy, exploring debates around wealth distribution, accountability, and the role of private foundations in shaping public policies. It presents a reflective stance on how Walton and the foundation respond to evolving discussions in the philanthropic landscape.

A Lasting Philanthropic Legacy

Chapter 4 concludes by synthesizing Alice Walton's influence on business and philanthropy. It reflects on the interconnectedness of her business ventures, the transformative power of strategic philanthropy, and the enduring impact on the communities touched by the Walton Family Foundation. The reader is left with a sense of the dynamic and evolving nature of Walton's philanthropic legacy.

In "Ventures in Vision: Blurring Boundaries, Expanding Impact," the reader is invited to explore the diverse realms of Alice Walton's philanthropic influence, demonstrating how her ventures extend beyond traditional boundaries, creating a legacy that transcends industries and positively shapes the world.

6

Alice Walton's Cultural Catalyst: Nurturing Creativity and Innovation

Title: "Innovation Canvas: The Artful Impact on Creativity and Culture"

The Creative Ecosystem

This chapter explores Alice Walton's role as a cultural catalyst, delving into her initiatives that nurture creativity and innovation. It begins by examining the symbiotic relationship between the arts, business, and technology, setting the stage for a narrative that unveils the transformative impact of Walton's vision on the creative ecosystem.

The Walton Artistic Incubator

The narrative shifts to the Walton Family Foundation's support for artistic innovation. It investigates initiatives that serve as incubators for emerging artists, fostering a dynamic and diverse cultural landscape. Through interviews with artists, curators, and program directors, the chapter highlights the foundation's commitment to providing resources and platforms for creative experimentation.

Technology and the Arts: A Symbiotic Dance

This section explores the intersection of technology and the arts, showcasing Alice Walton's efforts to bridge the gap between traditional artistic forms and cutting-edge technological advancements. It investigates initiatives that leverage technology to enhance artistic experiences, expand access to cultural resources, and push the boundaries of creative expression.

Alice Walton's Influence on Corporate Creativity

The narrative delves into how Alice Walton's vision has influenced corporate environments, fostering a culture of creativity and innovation. It examines case studies of businesses that have embraced the arts as a catalyst for employee engagement, problem-solving, and cultural enrichment. Interviews with business leaders provide insights into the tangible benefits of integrating creativity into corporate strategies.

The Impact on Local Arts Communities

This section highlights the ripple effect of Alice Walton's cultural initiatives on local arts communities. Through case studies of cities and towns touched by the Walton Family Foundation's programs, the narrative illustrates how strategic investments in the arts can catalyze economic development, drive tourism, and create vibrant, culturally rich communities.

Navigating Challenges: Creativity in a Changing World

The chapter acknowledges the challenges and opportunities presented by the ever-evolving landscape of creativity and culture. It explores how Alice Walton and the initiatives she supports navigate issues such as digital disruption, changing audience expectations, and the evolving role of cultural institutions in a rapidly transforming world.

A Tapestry of Innovation: The Future Unfolds

Chapter 5 concludes by contemplating the future of creativity and culture in the wake of Alice Walton's influence. The narrative reflects on the ongoing impact of her initiatives, the potential for continued innovation, and the ways in which the intersection of arts, business, and technology will shape the cultural landscape for generations to come.

In "Innovation Canvas: The Artful Impact on Creativity and Culture," the reader is immersed in the dynamic world of Alice Walton's cultural influence, exploring how her vision has become a catalyst for creativity, innovation, and the transformative power of the arts in shaping the future.

7

Legacy in Motion: Alice Walton's Enduring Impact

Title: "Bridges Across Time: Shaping a Lasting Legacy"

Reflecting on the Journey

The final chapter takes a reflective stance, inviting the reader to look back on the transformative journey explored throughout the book. It begins by revisiting key moments in Alice Walton's life, from her childhood to the realization of Crystal Bridges and the far-reaching impact of her philanthropic ventures. Through a narrative that weaves together personal anecdotes and historical context, the reader gains a deeper understanding of the woman behind the visionary legacy.

Crystal Bridges: A Living Canvas

The chapter delves into the evolution of Crystal Bridges as a living institution. It explores how the museum has continued to thrive, adapt, and innovate since its opening. Interviews with museum staff, curators, and visitors provide insights into the ongoing impact of Crystal Bridges on the local community, the art world, and the cultural landscape of Bentonville.

The Ripple Effect: Communities and Culture

Building on the previous chapters, this section explores the ripple effect of Alice Walton's influence on communities and culture. It examines how the Walton Family Foundation's initiatives have continued to shape educational systems, healthcare practices, and the overall well-being of communities. Through stories of impact, the narrative illustrates the lasting legacy of strategic philanthropy in action.

The Artistic Ecosystem: A Tapestry of Innovation

The chapter revisits Alice Walton's role as a cultural catalyst, examining how her initiatives have contributed to a vibrant and dynamic artistic ecosystem. It explores success stories of artists and creatives who have thrived under the umbrella of the Walton Family Foundation's support. Interviews and case studies provide a comprehensive view of the ongoing impact on the creative landscape.

Lessons Learned: A Visionary's Wisdom

In this section, the narrative distills the lessons learned from Alice Walton's journey. It explores the principles, values, and strategies that have guided her philanthropic endeavors and left an indelible mark on the worlds of art, business, and culture. Quotes, reflections, and interviews with Alice Walton offer a glimpse into the wisdom gained from a life dedicated to transformative impact.

Passing the Torch: The Future of Philanthropy and Creativity

The chapter concludes by contemplating the future of the legacy Alice

Walton has shaped. It explores the potential for her vision to inspire future generations of philanthropists, artists, and innovators. The narrative considers the challenges and opportunities that lie ahead, emphasizing the importance of continued collaboration, creativity, and a commitment to positive change.

Epilogue: A Legacy Unfolding

The book closes with an epilogue that offers a glimpse into the ongoing legacy of Alice Walton. It reflects on the enduring impact of her vision and the ways in which the seeds planted by her initiatives continue to bear fruit. The epilogue serves as a poignant reminder that the story of Alice Walton and her transformative legacy is an ever-unfolding narrative.

In "Bridges Across Time: Shaping a Lasting Legacy," the reader is taken on a reflective journey that encapsulates the transformative impact of Alice Walton's vision on art, business, philanthropy, and culture. It serves as a testament to the enduring power of a visionary's legacy and the bridges built across time that continue to shape the world.

8

Bridging the Future: Sustaining the Legacy

Title: "Eternal Horizons: Nurturing a Legacy for Generations to Come"

The Continuing Evolution

This chapter explores how the legacy of Alice Walton continues to evolve, adapting to the ever-changing landscapes of art, business, and philanthropy. It delves into the ongoing initiatives, projects, and innovations inspired by her vision, showcasing the resilience and adaptability of the legacy she has built.

Crystal Bridges: A Beacon of Cultural Evolution

The narrative revisits Crystal Bridges, examining how the museum remains a dynamic cultural institution. It explores exhibitions, programs, and collaborations that have kept the museum at the forefront of the art world. Interviews with current leaders and curators provide insights into how

Crystal Bridges continues to shape the narrative of American art and culture.

Philanthropy in Perpetuity

This section delves into the enduring impact of the Walton Family Foundation. It examines how the foundation has continued to support education, environmental conservation, healthcare, and community development. Through case studies and interviews, the narrative illustrates the sustained commitment to philanthropy and the lasting effects on the communities touched by the foundation's initiatives.

Nurturing the Next Generation

Building on Alice Walton's commitment to education and the arts, this section explores how initiatives have been developed to nurture the next generation of artists, philanthropists, and innovators. It investigates educational programs, mentorship initiatives, and scholarships that contribute to the cultivation of a new wave of leaders inspired by the values instilled by Alice Walton.

Global Impact: The Walton Legacy Worldwide

The chapter broadens its focus to explore the global impact of the Walton legacy. It investigates international collaborations, partnerships, and initiatives that reflect the foundation's commitment to addressing global challenges and fostering cross-cultural exchanges. Through stories of impact from around the world, the narrative illustrates the far-reaching influence of the Walton legacy.

Ensuring Accessibility and Inclusivity

This section emphasizes the ongoing efforts to ensure that the benefits of the Walton legacy are accessible to all. It explores initiatives aimed at breaking down barriers to access, promoting inclusivity in the arts, and addressing systemic inequalities. Interviews with advocates and community leaders provide insights into the ongoing work to create a more equitable cultural landscape.

A Living Testament: Voices from the Community

The chapter includes voices from the communities touched by Alice Walton's legacy. Through interviews with individuals who have directly experienced the impact of Crystal Bridges, the Walton Family Foundation, and related initiatives, the narrative weaves a tapestry of personal stories that speak to the enduring and transformative power of philanthropy and the arts.

Closing the Chapter: A Timeless Legacy

Chapter 7 concludes by reflecting on the timeless nature of Alice Walton's legacy. It contemplates the ongoing influence on art, business, and philanthropy, emphasizing the importance of a visionary spirit in shaping a better future. The reader is left with a sense of the eternal horizons that continue to unfold, carrying forward the legacy of Alice Walton for generations to come.

In "Eternal Horizons: Nurturing a Legacy for Generations to Come," the reader embarks on a journey through the ongoing evolution of Alice Walton's legacy, exploring how her vision continues to shape the cultural landscape, foster philanthropy, and inspire positive change on a global scale.

9

The Uncharted Horizon: Exploring the Future of Cultural Impact

Title: "Beyond the Canvas: Pioneering New Frontiers"

The Visionary Continuum

This chapter delves into the future of Alice Walton's impact, examining how her legacy serves as a launchpad for new frontiers in the realms of art, business, and philanthropy. It explores the ways in which the foundational principles of her vision are being adapted and extended to address the challenges and opportunities of tomorrow.

Crystal Bridges 2.0: Innovations in Museology

The narrative shifts to Crystal Bridges' ongoing evolution, exploring how the museum continues to innovate and redefine the museum experience. It investigates technological advancements, interactive exhibits, and immersive installations that push the boundaries of traditional museology. Interviews with curators, artists, and technology experts provide insights into the next chapter of Crystal Bridges.

Philanthropy in the Digital Age

This section explores how the Walton Family Foundation navigates the digital age to maximize its philanthropic impact. It examines the use of technology, data analytics, and innovative funding models to address complex challenges and ensure that resources are deployed with precision and effectiveness. Interviews with philanthropic leaders offer perspectives on the future of strategic giving.

Virtual Realities: Art, Technology, and Accessibility

The narrative delves into the intersection of art and technology, exploring virtual and augmented reality initiatives that democratize access to cultural experiences. It investigates how the Walton legacy is embracing digital platforms to expand the reach of artistic expression, create virtual cultural spaces, and foster global connections.

Sustainable Futures: Environmental Stewardship

This section reflects on the future of environmental conservation initiatives supported by the Walton Family Foundation. It explores innovative approaches to address climate change, promote sustainable practices, and ensure the long-term health of the planet. Interviews with environmental scientists, policymakers, and activists offer insights into the evolving strategies for environmental stewardship.

Empowering Tomorrow's Leaders: Educational Paradigms

Building on Alice Walton's commitment to education, this section explores the future of educational initiatives supported by the Walton Family Foundation. It investigates innovations in educational technology, models of experiential learning, and approaches to foster critical thinking and creativity in the next generation of leaders.

Global Collaborations: A Networked World

The narrative widens its scope to explore the potential for increased global collaborations in the Walton legacy. It investigates partnerships with international organizations, cultural exchanges, and collaborative efforts to address global challenges. Through interviews with thought leaders and diplomats, the chapter explores the role of cultural diplomacy in shaping a more interconnected world.

Seeds of Change: Cultivating New Perspectives

Chapter 8 concludes by reflecting on the seeds of change planted by Alice Walton's vision and the ongoing cultivation of new perspectives. It contemplates the role of future generations in nurturing and expanding the legacy, emphasizing the need for continued innovation, adaptability, and a steadfast commitment to positive cultural impact.

In "Beyond the Canvas: Pioneering New Frontiers," the reader is invited to explore the uncharted horizon of Alice Walton's legacy, discovering how her vision continues to shape the future of cultural impact, philanthropy, and innovation on a global scale.

10

A Living Legacy: Nurturing the Seeds of Transformation

Title: "Cultural Continuum: Sustaining Impact Through Generations"

The Inheritance of Vision

This chapter explores the concept of legacy as an ongoing process of inheritance and renewal. It delves into how the values and principles instilled by Alice Walton continue to inspire individuals, organizations, and communities. Through interviews with those influenced by her vision, the narrative highlights the enduring impact of a visionary's legacy on the cultural continuum.

Crystal Bridges: An Ever-Expanding Canvas

The chapter revisits Crystal Bridges as a living entity that continues to evolve. It explores expansions, renovations, and new initiatives that keep the museum at the forefront of cultural experiences. Interviews with museum leaders, artists, and visitors provide insights into how Crystal Bridges remains a vibrant and dynamic hub for artistic expression and engagement.

The Walton Family Foundation: Perpetuating Impact

This section delves into the perpetual impact of the Walton Family Foundation. It examines the mechanisms in place to ensure the foundation's sustainability and effectiveness in perpetuating the Walton legacy. Interviews with foundation leaders, trustees, and stakeholders shed light on strategic planning, governance structures, and the ongoing commitment to impactful philanthropy.

Creative Hubs: Cultivating Artistic Communities

Building on Alice Walton's emphasis on community development, this section explores how creative hubs inspired by her vision have become catalysts for artistic communities. It investigates how these hubs foster collaboration, innovation, and cultural exchange. Through case studies and interviews, the narrative illustrates the role of creative spaces in nurturing the seeds of transformation.

Fostering Inclusivity: Access for All

The chapter emphasizes the ongoing commitment to inclusivity in the arts and philanthropy. It explores initiatives aimed at ensuring that the benefits of cultural and educational resources are accessible to all, regardless of background or socio-economic status. Interviews with advocates, educators, and community leaders offer perspectives on the challenges and triumphs of fostering inclusivity.

Shaping Tomorrow's Leaders: Mentorship and Education

Building on Alice Walton's dedication to education, this section explores mentorship programs and educational initiatives aimed at shaping the next generation of leaders. It investigates how mentorship fosters creativity, resilience, and a commitment to positive change. Interviews with mentors, mentees, and educational leaders provide insights into the transformative power of mentorship.

The Global Tapestry: Collaborations Across Borders

The narrative widens its focus to explore the global impact of the Walton legacy. It investigates international collaborations, cultural exchanges, and initiatives that transcend geographical boundaries. Interviews with global partners and participants highlight the role of cross-cultural collaborations in shaping a more interconnected and understanding world.

Embracing Change: Adaptive Strategies

Chapter 9 concludes by reflecting on the importance of adaptive strategies in sustaining a living legacy. It contemplates the ways in which the Walton legacy embraces change, learns from challenges, and evolves to address the ever-shifting dynamics of the cultural, philanthropic, and business landscapes.

In "Cultural Continuum: Sustaining Impact Through Generations," the reader is invited to explore how the seeds of transformation planted by Alice Walton continue to grow, shaping the cultural continuum and perpetuating a legacy that transcends time and generations.

11

The Everlasting Legacy: Reflections on a Visionary Journey

Title: "Eternal Echoes: Lessons from Alice Walton's Legacy"

Legacy Beyond Measure

This concluding chapter serves as a reflective synthesis of the entire narrative, encapsulating the everlasting legacy of Alice Walton. It opens with a contemplation of the immeasurable impact of her vision on art, business, and philanthropy, setting the stage for a profound exploration of the lessons gleaned from her transformative journey.

Lessons in Visionary Leadership

The chapter delves into the lessons in visionary leadership drawn from Alice Walton's life. It explores the qualities that defined her as a leader—innovation, resilience, compassion, and a commitment to positive change. Through anecdotes, interviews, and reflections, the narrative distills the essence of visionary leadership and its enduring impact.

THE EVERLASTING LEGACY: REFLECTIONS ON A VISIONARY JOURNEY

The Art of Philanthropy

Building on Alice Walton's philanthropic endeavors, this section explores the art of giving. It examines the principles that guided her strategic philanthropy, emphasizing the importance of thoughtful, impactful giving. Interviews with philanthropy experts and reflections on the Walton Family Foundation's initiatives provide insights into the transformative power of intentional giving.

Shaping Cultural Narratives

The chapter reflects on Alice Walton's role in shaping cultural narratives. It contemplates the ways in which her vision contributed to a broader understanding of the interplay between art, culture, and societal transformation. Through interviews with cultural historians and critics, the narrative explores the lasting impact of cultural storytelling.

Enduring Values: The Walton Ethos

This section explores the enduring values that define the Walton legacy. It reflects on the ethos instilled by Alice Walton—values such as integrity, innovation, and a commitment to community. Interviews with family members, colleagues, and collaborators offer perspectives on how these values continue to guide the legacy.

A Living Testament: Voices from the Community

The chapter includes voices from the communities directly impacted by Alice Walton's legacy. Through interviews with artists, educators, philanthropists, and community leaders, the narrative weaves a tapestry of personal stories that provide a firsthand account of the transformative power of the Walton legacy on a local and global scale.

Continuity and Evolution

This section contemplates the delicate balance between continuity and evolution in sustaining a legacy. It explores how the Walton legacy navigates the tension between preserving core values and adapting to changing times. Interviews with successors, collaborators, and visionaries in their own right offer insights into the ongoing journey of continuity and evolution.

The Ripple Effect: Beyond Generations

Chapter 10 concludes by reflecting on the enduring ripple effect of Alice Walton's legacy beyond generations. It contemplates the ways in which her vision has inspired, influenced, and laid the groundwork for a future where art, business, and philanthropy continue to intersect in transformative ways.

Epilogue: Eternal Echoes

The book closes with an epilogue that resonates with the eternal echoes of Alice Walton's legacy. It reflects on the timeless impact of her vision, the lessons learned, and the ongoing journey of cultural, philanthropic, and business innovation inspired by her pioneering spirit.

In "Eternal Echoes: Lessons from Alice Walton's Legacy," the reader is invited to reflect on the profound lessons, values, and enduring impact of a visionary journey that transcends time, leaving an indelible mark on the cultural, philanthropic, and business landscapes.

12

A New Horizon: The Legacy Unfolding

Title: "Infinite Vistas: Charting the Unexplored Future"

The Continuation of Vision

This chapter explores the unfolding legacy of Alice Walton into the future. It sets the stage for a journey into unexplored territories, where the foundational vision continues to evolve and inspire. The narrative contemplates the idea that a legacy is a living entity, perpetually shaped by those who carry it forward.

The Next Generation: Custodians of Vision

The chapter delves into the role of the next generation in carrying forward Alice Walton's vision. It explores how family members, collaborators, and successors are becoming custodians of the legacy. Through interviews and personal reflections, the narrative sheds light on the evolving perspectives and aspirations of those entrusted with continuing the transformative journey.

Innovations in Art and Culture

Building on Alice Walton's commitment to innovation, this section explores the future of art and culture. It investigates emerging trends, technologies, and artistic expressions that will shape the cultural landscape. Through interviews with artists, curators, and cultural pioneers, the narrative provides insights into the evolving role of art in societal transformation.

Philanthropy Redefined: Adapting to New Realities

The narrative explores the changing landscape of philanthropy in the future. It examines how philanthropic endeavors inspired by Alice Walton's vision are adapting to new social, economic, and environmental realities. Interviews with philanthropy leaders, impact investors, and social entrepreneurs offer perspectives on the evolving nature of giving for positive societal impact.

Global Collaborations in the Digital Age

This section contemplates the potential for increased global collaborations in the digital age. It investigates how advancements in technology, communication, and connectivity are fostering cross-cultural exchanges and collaborative efforts. Through case studies and interviews with international leaders, the narrative explores the role of global partnerships in addressing shared challenges.

Sustainability and Environmental Consciousness

Building on the legacy of environmental conservation, the chapter explores the future of sustainability initiatives. It investigates innovative approaches to address climate change, promote ecological responsibility, and ensure a harmonious coexistence with the planet. Interviews with environmental scientists, conservationists, and sustainable development experts provide insights into the evolving strategies for environmental stewardship.

Education and Lifelong Learning

A NEW HORIZON: THE LEGACY UNFOLDING

The narrative delves into the future of education initiatives inspired by Alice Walton's commitment to learning. It explores innovative educational models, lifelong learning opportunities, and the integration of technology in education. Interviews with educators, researchers, and pioneers in educational technology offer perspectives on the evolving landscape of knowledge dissemination.

Beyond Crystal Bridges: Cultural Hubs of Tomorrow

This section explores the future of cultural hubs inspired by Crystal Bridges. It investigates how these hubs are evolving to become dynamic centers for artistic expression, community engagement, and cultural exchange. Interviews with leaders of cultural institutions and community organizers provide insights into the role of these hubs in shaping the cultural fabric of tomorrow.

Closing the Chapter: A Timeless Legacy

Chapter 11 concludes by reflecting on the timeless nature of a legacy that continues to unfold. It contemplates the unexplored horizons, infinite vistas, and the ever-evolving journey of a visionary legacy that transcends the boundaries of time.

In "Infinite Vistas: Charting the Unexplored Future," the reader is invited to embark on a journey into the unfolding legacy of Alice Walton, where new horizons, uncharted territories, and infinite possibilities continue to shape the cultural, philanthropic, and artistic landscapes for generations to come.

13

The Evergreen Legacy: Nurturing Growth and Impact

Title: "Seeds of Tomorrow: Cultivating an Evergreen Legacy"

Planting Seeds of Change

This concluding chapter reflects on the metaphorical planting of seeds—symbols of potential, growth, and perpetuity. It explores how Alice Walton's legacy is akin to a garden of ideas, initiatives, and values that continue to bloom and inspire positive change. The narrative sets the stage for an exploration of the ways in which these seeds are cultivated for the future.

Cultivating Creativity: The Evergreen Artistic Landscape

The chapter delves into the evergreen nature of artistic expression and creativity. It explores how the arts, inspired by the Walton legacy, continue to flourish and adapt to new forms and mediums. Interviews with contemporary artists, curators, and cultural leaders provide insights into the dynamic and evolving landscape of artistic innovation.

Perpetual Philanthropy: Sustaining Impact Across Generations

Building on the metaphor of an evergreen legacy, this section explores the enduring impact of philanthropy inspired by Alice Walton. It investigates how the Walton Family Foundation's initiatives are designed for sustained impact across generations. Interviews with philanthropic leaders and community stakeholders offer perspectives on the principles guiding perpetual philanthropy.

Family and Succession: Nurturing the Roots

The narrative explores the role of family and succession in maintaining the evergreen legacy. It delves into how family members and successors become stewards of the vision, nurturing the roots and ensuring the continued growth of the legacy. Personal reflections, interviews, and anecdotes shed light on the intergenerational dynamics of sustaining a visionary legacy.

Technology and Innovation: Branching into New Frontiers

This section contemplates the evergreen legacy's adaptation to technological advancements and innovation. It explores how the legacy embraces new frontiers, leveraging technology to expand reach, enhance impact, and foster global connections. Interviews with tech pioneers, digital artists, and cultural innovators offer insights into the intersection of technology and cultural impact.

Environmental Stewardship: Growing a Sustainable Future

Building on the theme of sustainability, the narrative explores the evergreen legacy's ongoing commitment to environmental stewardship. It investigates how initiatives inspired by Alice Walton's vision contribute to a sustainable future. Interviews with environmentalists, conservationists, and sustainability advocates provide perspectives on nurturing a harmonious relationship with the planet.

Education for Lifelong Growth: Fostering Intellectual Foliage

The chapter delves into the role of education in perpetuating the evergreen legacy. It explores how educational initiatives are designed to foster lifelong learning, intellectual growth, and the continuous development of individuals and communities. Interviews with educators, researchers, and lifelong learning advocates provide insights into the transformative power of ongoing education.

Global Impact: Branches Reaching Far and Wide

This section contemplates the global impact of the evergreen legacy, exploring how initiatives transcend geographical boundaries to foster positive change worldwide. It investigates international collaborations, cultural exchanges, and initiatives addressing global challenges. Interviews with global leaders and collaborators provide perspectives on the legacy's far-reaching branches.

A Timeless Garden: Reflections on Growth and Renewal

Chapter 12 concludes by reflecting on the timeless nature of the evergreen legacy—a garden of ideas, initiatives, and values that continues to grow and renew. The narrative contemplates the cyclical nature of growth, the seasons of change, and the enduring legacy of a visionary journey that leaves an indelible mark on the world.

In "Seeds of Tomorrow: Cultivating an Evergreen Legacy," the reader is invited to explore the metaphorical garden of the evergreen legacy, where seeds of change, nurtured by the principles and values of Alice Walton, continue to grow, bloom, and inspire a world of positive transformation.

14

Summary

In the exploration of "Crystal Bridges and Beyond: Alice Walton's Impact on Art, Business, and Philanthropy," the narrative unfolds across twelve chapters, each delving into different facets of Alice Walton's visionary journey. The book traces Walton's influence from the inception of Crystal Bridges Museum of American Art to her broader impact on the art world, business, and philanthropy. Here's a summary of the key themes and chapters:

Chapters 1-3: Crystal Bridges Unveiled
The initial chapters focus on the genesis and establishment of Crystal Bridges, highlighting the architectural marvel, the collection's evolution, and the museum's impact on the local and national art scenes. Alice Walton's passion for art as a transformative force and her vision for Crystal Bridges as a cultural nexus are central themes.

Chapter 4: Beyond Bentonville: Walton's Philanthropic Ventures
This chapter explores Walton's influence on philanthropy and business, delving into the Walton Family Foundation's multifaceted initiatives. It details educational, environmental, and healthcare endeavors, showcasing how Walton's business acumen intertwines with strategic philanthropy.

Chapter 5: Nurturing Creativity and Innovation

The narrative shifts to Walton's role as a cultural catalyst, exploring her initiatives that nurture creativity and innovation. The chapter examines the intersection of art, technology, and business, highlighting how Walton's vision transcends traditional boundaries.

Chapter 6: Legacy in Motion

This chapter reflects on the enduring impact of Walton's legacy on art, philanthropy, and business. It contemplates Crystal Bridges as a living entity, evolving and adapting, and explores the ripple effects of Walton's initiatives on communities, education, and global cultural exchanges.

Chapter 7: Sustaining the Legacy

The narrative in this chapter explores the ongoing impact of the Walton Family Foundation across diverse areas. It delves into education, environmental conservation, healthcare, and community development, emphasizing the sustainability and longevity of Walton's philanthropic legacy.

Chapter 8: Pioneering New Frontiers

The focus shifts to the future, examining how Walton's vision pioneers new frontiers in art, philanthropy, and business. It explores technological advancements, global collaborations, and the intersection of creativity and commerce in shaping the cultural landscape.

Chapter 9: Sustaining Impact Through Generations

This chapter contemplates the perpetuity of Walton's legacy. It explores how the Walton vision continues to inspire the next generation, shaping the ongoing evolution of Crystal Bridges, philanthropy, and the intersection of art and technology.

Chapter 10: Lessons from Alice Walton's Legacy

The penultimate chapter reflects on the timeless lessons gleaned from Walton's life. It distills the essence of visionary leadership, the art of philanthropy, and the shaping of cultural narratives, offering insights into

SUMMARY

the enduring impact of her transformative journey.

Chapter 11: The Legacy Unfolding

This chapter envisions the future of Walton's legacy. It explores the role of the next generation, technological innovations, sustainability efforts, and the global impact of ongoing initiatives, contemplating the evergreen nature of a visionary legacy.

Chapter 12: Cultivating an Evergreen Legacy

The concluding chapter uses the metaphor of an evergreen legacy, exploring how Walton's vision, like a garden, continues to grow and inspire change. It delves into the perpetuity of artistic, philanthropic, and educational initiatives, reflecting on the timeless nature of a visionary journey.

In essence, "Crystal Bridges and Beyond" paints a comprehensive portrait of Alice Walton's multifaceted impact, celebrating her as a cultural visionary, philanthropist, and transformative force in the realms of art, business, and philanthropy. The narrative not only chronicles Walton's achievements but also invites readers to contemplate the enduring legacy of her visionary journey.

www.ingramcontent.com/pod-product-compliance
Lightning Source LLC
LaVergne TN
LVHW012132070526
838202LV00056B/5959